How to Fix a Leak

and Other Household Plumbing Projects

TEXT BY DEANNE RAFFEL

WALLABY

A WALLABY BOOK
Published by Simon & Schuster
New York

Published by WALLABY BOOKS
A Simon & Schuster Division of
GULF & WESTERN CORPORATION
Simon & Schuster Building
1230 Avenue of the Americas
New York, New York 10020

WALLABY and colophon are trademarks
of Simon & Schuster

First Wallaby Books Printing May, 1981

10 9 8 7 6 5 4 3 2 1

Manufactured in the United States of America

Library of Congress Catalogue Card Number: 80-26506

ISBN: 0-671-42307-X

The advice in this book is based on careful research
and analysis. Due care should be taken in any repair
or maintenance program. The author and publisher
cannot take any responsibility for damage or injuries
caused by repairs or maintenance performed by
the reader.

Production: Jeffrey Weiss Group, Inc./Color Book Design, Inc.
Series Editor: Edward P. Stevenson
Design: Deborah Bracken, Design Director
Design Consultant: Robert Luzzi
Managing Editor: Barbara Frontera
Copy Chief: Donna Florence
Illustrated by: Robert Strimban
Special Thanks to Jack Artenstein, Eugene Brissie, Jenny Doctorow and
Channa Taub

Table of Contents

Introduction

It's a cliché—like the Chinese water torture, a dripping faucet can drive you half out of your mind. But most of us are programmed only to go on futilely tightening the handle harder and harder, grinding our teeth and muttering curses under our breath. Meanwhile, the faucet goes right on dripping and the water bill mounting. Getting a plumber in "just to fix a faucet" is next to impossible these days. And if you *do* get a plumber to come, you set up a classic situation: as long as he's there anyway, the plumber may try to convince you that the faucet is simply "worn out" and needs to be replaced. This is usually a losing battle for your side, and whatever the outcome, it can be expensive.

Good news! Fixing a faucet is not a job for a plumber—not

these days, anyway, when a plumber's time costs upwards of $25 an hour. Armed with the proper tools, accurate information, and a little confidence, you can make most faucet and other simple plumbing repairs in less time than you would spend persuading a plumber to come—and at a fraction of the cost. The tools are easily acquired at a modest cost and the other ingredients, information and confidence, can be obtained just as easily—by reading this book.

On the following pages you will find a number of simple but common and *necessary* plumbing repairs that you can perform easily. They include most of the major problem areas where leaks and drips occur: in pipes, pipe joints and at valves of faucets and toilets. Your whole household plumbing system (both supply and drainage pipes) is described and illustrated; the necessary tools are discussed; and thorough step-by-step instructions are accompanied by clear drawings for each repair and project. Read *all* of the book before attempting to make any plumbing repairs. It will give you a broad understanding of the problems involved, and of the tools and materials you will need to use. Then reread the text for the problem area you are dealing with, study the illustrations carefully, make sure you have the necessary tools on hand and go to work, following *all* instructions, in sequence.

Most simple, basic parts can be purchased at your local hardware store. If you can't find what you need there, try a large do-it-yourself home improvement center or a plumbing supply house. Don't be intimidated by the plumbing supply house. In addition to being able to provide you with a truly full selection of available parts, the dealer there is actually your most reliable source of supplementary *information*.

You will find that some leaks take very little time to fix—they require only the tightening of a nut or the replacement of a small part—while others may take more time and thought. But once you are "into it," you will enjoy being your own plumber. And, unless you are very unusual, you will get great *satisfaction* from it.

Your Home Plumbing System

The plumbing system in your home actually consists of *two separate* systems: 1) an intake or fresh water **supply** system, and, 2) an outlet or **drainage** system that empties through a large waste pipe leading to a municipal sewer, septic tank or cesspool.

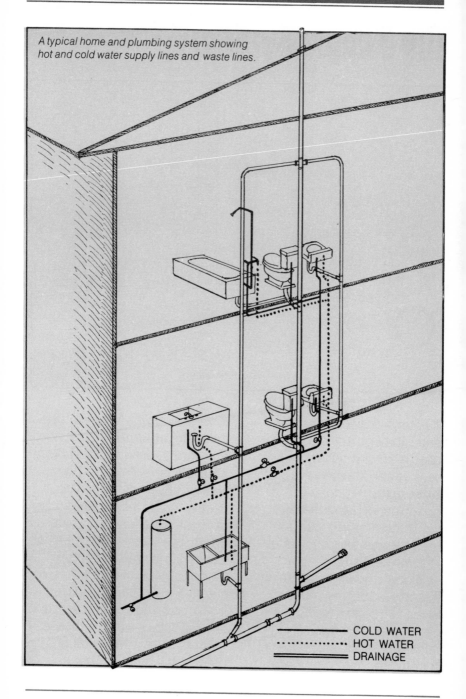

A typical home and plumbing system showing hot and cold water supply lines and waste lines.

COLD WATER
HOT WATER
DRAINAGE

7

The Supply System

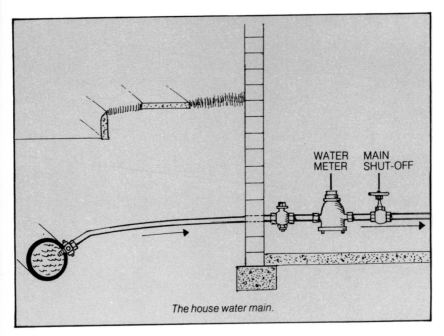

WATER METER   MAIN SHUT-OFF

The house water main.

All water supplied to a house comes through a single pipe called the main house supply line, also called simply the **house main**. It is located underground, below the frost line; it runs into the house from the street where it is connected to the **street main**.

Inside the house there are (or there *should* be) a number of **valves** that control the flow of water to the various parts of the house. Just inside the house or property line, before the main

flows through the water meter is the **meter shut-off** valve. Inside from the meter is the main **house shut-off** valve. From the house shut-off, the main supply line usually runs to the furnace, boiler or water heater where it divides to form two lines—one for the hot water, one for the cold water. From this point, the hot and cold supply lines branch out to feed the fixtures and appliances that require water all over the house.

There *should* be a number of branch shut-off valves controlling the water lines as they lead to the various parts of the dwelling. A house with proper and adequate plumbing has a set of such **water line stop valves** (or "line stops") leading to each general plumbing area of the house—kitchen, laundry room, bathrooms—as well as to the furnace or boiler and the water heater. These valves should be *accessible*, and you should *know where they are*. It should be possible for you to shut off the water supply to any area of the house in which there might be a leak, or in which plumbing repairs are being carried out, *without* cutting off the water supply to the rest of the house.

In addition to line stops, most up-to-date plumbing install-ations provide **fixture stops**, which control the flow of hot and cold water from the water supply lines to each individual fixture (faucet, toilet, appliance, etc.). It is easier to shut off a fixture stop when changing a faucet washer than to track down the appropriate line stop or shut off all the water in the house at the main.

It is a good idea to find and tag all the stop valves in your water supply system. (Fixture stops shouldn't need tags; they are located directly adjacent to, and are directly connected to, the fixtures they serve.) Indicate on each line stop the areas or fixtures that the valve controls. (Do this for *all* line stop valves, including the ones leading to the boiler and water heater. Water supply systems can be visually confusing.)

Also be sure everyone in your household knows the location of the **main shut-off**, and be sure they all understand the importance of this valve in an emergency situation: it is the *one sure means* of shutting off the water when there is a leak. If you can go straight to the main, you don't have to fumble with line stop valves, guessing which is the right one. You can stop the leak *fast* and get the details sorted out later on.

The Drainage System

Water wastes from the household originating at each plumbing fixture or water-using appliance empty into the septic system or municipal sewer via a system of drainage pipes in your house. Some of these pipes, the larger ones (up to 6 inches in diameter), are called **soil pipes** and carry human wastes from toilets (properly called "water closets" in plumbing lingo). The rest, relatively small (1½ to 2½ inches in diameter), carry used water from other fixtures such as sinks, lavatories, tubs, washers, etc. and are called **waste pipes**.

The soil lines and waste lines from each level of your home are joined together by horizontal and vertical runs of pipe. ("Horizontal" runs are not truly horizontal, but pitched downward, away from the fixtures, in the direction of the main drainage so that liquids will flow efficiently.) Vertical runs of drainage pipes are called **stacks**. Depending on what a given stack drains, it may be a small waste stack or a larger soil stack. (Any *soil* line must always drain into a line or stack *at least* as big as itself.) Eventually, all the soil and waste lines and stacks come together in the main house drain or house sewer, which empties into the municipal sewer or septic system.

Beside the pipes through which the liquid wastes drain away, there is an additional set of pipes that rise up through the roof and bring a supply of fresh air to the drainage pipes. Called **vents**, these prevent any problems in the system that might result from unequal pressures: either vacuums or positive pressure buildups. Vent stacks are basically upward extensions of the waste and soil stacks but do not carry any water, only air and, occasionally, other gases. Without vent lines, waste and water would not flow safely and properly through your home's drainage system. They are mentioned here not because you are likely ever to do any work on them, but so that you will be aware of their presence and function and will thus understand your total plumbing system better.

Perhaps the most important elements in the drainage system, from the health and safety point of view, are the numerous **traps**. A trap associated with each plumbing fixture in your home effects an airtight seal between the inside of the sewer system and the inside of your home. A trap is merely a U shaped bend of pipe (or some mechanical equivalent of that) and the seal is made by water. The water sitting in the U bend serves as a barrier to prevent sewer gases from "backing up" through the drainage system into your house. Since the whole system is

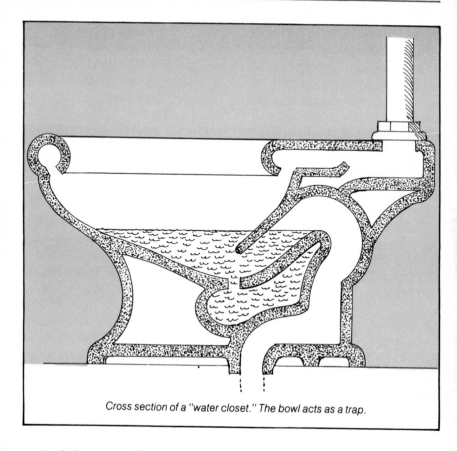

Cross section of a "water closet." The bowl acts as a trap.

vented, the gases, if any, have an easy route to follow—up the vent stack to the outdoors, not into your rooms.

Every plumbing fixture has a trap. It is usually a built-in part of the drain itself. Traps for kitchen sinks and lavatories are made in two shapes: the "P" and the "S," depending on whether the drain pipe runs horizontally or vertically. The **J bend** is a component in both styles and is easily replaced if it wears out or is broken. Most bathtubs and showers have **P traps**, but they are not generally accessible. In some bathrooms a special shower or tub trap called a **drum trap** is used. It is accessible through a round plate visible on the bathroom floor. Your toilet bowl is a trap in and of itself as you can see by looking at this cross-section. There is one more important trap: the **main house**

trap, a large U bend in the house sewer, just inside the house. The main house trap is properly (and almost invariably) equipped with some sort of **cleanouts**, or access hatches, so that blockages can be removed.

Checking for Water Waste

If you have a large water bill in spite of being conservative in your water use, there are probably some dripping and leaking plumbing fixtures around your house. Plumbing leaks are nothing new, but as we become increasingly aware of the finite, non-renewable nature of the world-water supply, it becomes increasingly important that we use the resource wisely and waste as little as possible. The amount of water wasted by un-noticed plumbing leaks may seem insignificant, but if you knew what proportion of your water bill went for water you didn't even use, you would probably be more concerned.

Most plumbing leaks do go unnoticed, but there is a simple way to find out if you *do* have leaks. First, turn off *all* of the water-using fixtures and appliances in the house. This includes things you don't normally think about, such as refrigerators with automatic ice makers and heating systems with automatic humidifiers or refill systems. Next, go to your water meter and note the positions of *all* dials, numbers or calibrations. After an hour, come back and read the meter again. If there has been any change in the meter reading, you either forgot to turn off some appliance or, more probably, you have leaks.

You will want to ferret out all of the leaks, apparent *or* hidden—water loss is costly and wasteful, *and* some leaks can damage your house. The two major culprits are dripping faucets and "running" toilets. Of course a dripping faucet is easy to spot, but a toilet that wastes water may be less obvious. Ways to discover silent toilet leaks will be dealt with in the section on toilet repairs.

But there may be other leaks that are not only silent but invisible. If you know that all your faucets and all your toilets are leak-free, and the water meter test still reveals water loss somewhere in your supply system, you will have to look further. There may be leakage around valve connections, at pipe connections inside the walls, or at virtually any point in your supply system. Examine all the visible parts of the system—all the places where fresh water supply pipes are exposed. Eventually, leaks inside the walls or floors will show up as water spots in your walls and ceilings. This type of leak is much more difficult to pinpoint and to repair and will probably call for a visit by a plumber. But don't ignore them. They won't go away, they will only get *worse* and do increasing damage to your house.

Tools You Will Need

When you do any type of repair or installation work in your home, you will find that having the proper tools for a job makes for ease and expediency. This is especially true when doing plumbing work. Although there are many household tools that do several jobs, some particular tools will be needed as additions to your toolbox. When acquiring or replacing tools, beware! There are many inferior grade tools on the market that are poorly machined and cast from low-grade steel. Do not be tempted to waste your money on such tools. They do not stand up well under use, nor do they usually work well in the first place. Purchase well-made tools. They are more costly initially, but well worth the investment—and cheaper in the long run.

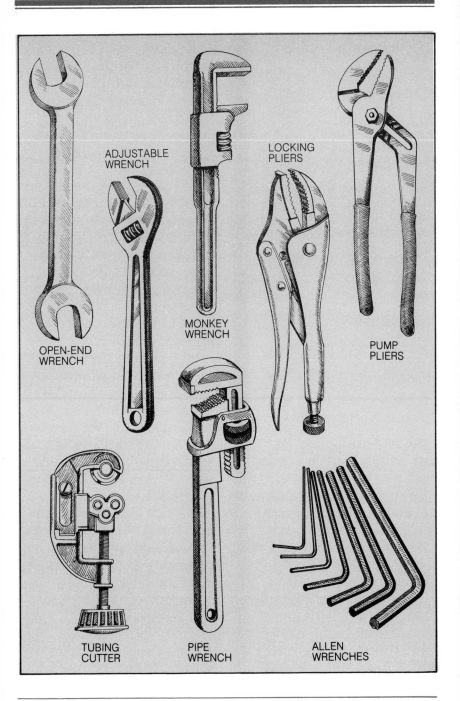

ADJUSTABLE
WRENCH

LOCKING
PLIERS

OPEN-END
WRENCH

MONKEY
WRENCH

PUMP
PLIERS

TUBING
CUTTER

PIPE
WRENCH

ALLEN
WRENCHES

You will need the following tools to do plumbing work:

- 12-inch adjustable wrench or "monkey" wrench

- 10-inch pipe wrench

- a pair of 12-inch slip-joint "pump" pliers

- a pair of locking or "grip" pliers

- a standard set of open-end *or* a 6-inch adjustable wrench

- standard-blade and Phillips-head screwdrivers in a variety of sizes

- a pocket knife ·

In addition, you may need:

- a set of Allen wrenches (hex keys)

- a hacksaw or tubing cutter

Most of these tools are designed to grip and turn nuts and pipes of various sizes in various situations. The 12-inch adjustable wrench is a very versatile tool. Its jaws will accomodate nuts of a number of moderate sizes. The offset angle of the head of the typical adjustable wrench makes it possible to get leverage on nuts that you wouldn't otherwise be able to reach. The monkey wrench is similar to the adjustable "cres-cent" wrench in most respects except that its jaws are perpendicular to the handle. The large "pump" pliers are good for turning large-diameter nuts such as the slip nuts on sink traps, etc. The locking pliers are an invaluable second pair of hands in many situations.

A set of open-end wrenches is handy in situations where you are working with several different-sized nuts in the same job and you don't want to keep adjusting your adjustable wrench. The smaller adjustable is a perfectly good substitute, and handy for tight spaces where a bigger wrench would not fit.

The pipe wrench is a different animal altogether. Its movable offset jaws grip pipes or other round objects by means of a crimping action once torque has been applied and the teeth have attained a purchase. Since the teeth of the pipe wrench do bite into the pipe in the normal course of use, if the pipe wrenches are used on chrome-plated or other visible pipes, the pipes must be protected with tape to prevent scars and damage.

Hex keys or Allen wrenches are called in for plumbing mostly to loosen small set screws, such as those that fasten handles to faucets. A larger Allen wrench may also be used to remove a replaceable faucet seat. If you should have to cut a piece of tubing in the course of your plumbing repair work, you will need either a hacksaw or a tubing cutter. Hacksaws are fairly familiar tools and many households already contain one. The tubing is a handy alternative for cutting *copper* tubing, which is what the typical fixture supply tubing is, underneath the chrome plating.

The tubing cutter is easy to use. The cutting wheel is adjusted by means of a screw so the pipe just fits. The wheel is then lightly tightened against the pipe and the whole cutter revolved around the pipe. The wheel will score a neat line in the pipe. The wheel is then tightened a bit more and the cutter revolved around the pipe a few more turns. This procedure is repeated—tighten, cut, tighten, cut—until the tubing is severed neatly.

Materials

In addition to the tools mentioned above, you will need several other very basic materials that are found around most homes. Their uses are reasonably obvious.

• sponge

• rags

• newspapers

• steel wool

• bucket

Finally, a few specific plumbing supplies will be called for:

• an assortment of faucet washers, O rings, and other replacement faucet parts

• a roll of Teflon tape for sealing pipe threads

Special tools or materials that may be needed for particular repairs will be mentioned in the appropriate place in the sections dealing with those repairs.

Emergency Leak Repairs

Usually, when a pipe starts to leak, more leaks will surely follow and the section should be replaced—especially in old brass or galvanized plumbing. Until you can call a plumber, there are a few emergency measures that may stop the leaking for the time being. Before attempting any repair, always turn off the water at the nearest stop valve, let the pipe drain and wipe the surface dry.

A continually wet spot, in the absence of an obvious leak, means that there is a pinhole opening where water can escape. Use a flashlight to locate it. If you can't find the hole, dry

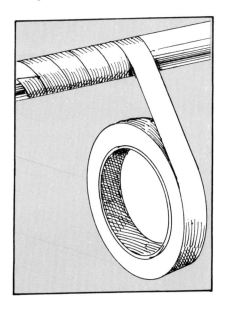

the pipe thoroughly and wrap several layers of vinyl tape over the area (work about 3" to each side of the wet spot). Pull the tape taut with each pass of the roll. If you *can* see the hole, use a round toothpick to plug it. Break the toothpick in half and drive it into the hole by tapping lightly with a tool or wood scrap. Break off the projecting end of the toothpick (if you can) and wrap the repair with tape as above.

If the hole is larger than a pinhead, use a short, small self-tapping galvanized sheet metal screw to close it off. Cut a small gasket from a piece of rubber (cut from an old inner tube) or flexible plastic, and insert the screw into its center. Place the screw tip over the hole and drive the screw with a screwdriver into the pipe until it is securely against the pipe wall. (The smaller the screw, the less it will interfere with the flow of water within the pipe.)

A larger leak needs clamping leverage. Cut a rubber patch,

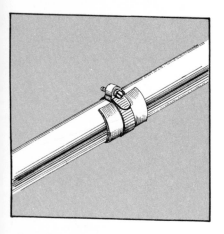

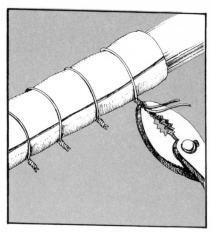

place it over the leak, and clamp tightly with a worm-drive hose clamp. A section of garden hose

clamps to secure it. If the clamps aren't readily available, wire can also be used to secure the sleeve. Use a C-clamp as a last

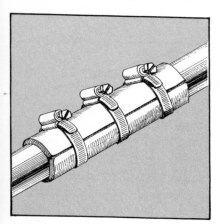

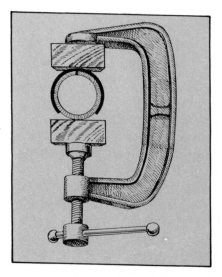

also makes a good patch. Split the hose lengthwise to slip it over the pipe. Use three worm-drive

resort method for sealing the leak. Hold a piece of rubber over the leak and sandwich the pipe between two pieces of soft wood so as not to exert too much pressure on the weakened section. Be careful! This is a tricky solution and temporary at best. Do not overtighten the clamp or the pipe will *really* leak!

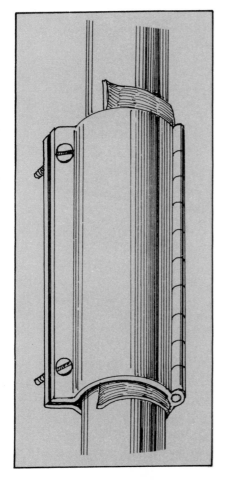

A commercial pipe sleeve will serve to patch a leak if you don't

plan to have the section re- placed in the near future. The clamp has a pin running down its back like a hinge and a rubber sleeve that hugs the pipe when the nuts are tightened to the machine screws. (Be sure that you know the pipe diameter when purchasing the sleeve. They are sized according to the outside diameters of the pipes, whereas pipe sizes are often re- ferred to by their *inside* diameter.)

Many times all that is neces- sary to stop a leak at a pipe joint fitting is to tighten a nut. If tighten- ing a nut doesn't do the job (or if the joint is soldered), try using a sealer. Open a faucet down the line from the joint to drain the pipe. Wipe the area dry, blow into it to force any moisture out. Swab the joint with epoxy ce- ment or epoxy plumbing repair putty. The cement or putty must cure before the water pressure is restored.

There is one other kind of pipe leak that actually is not a leak at all; it's sweating pipes. Sweating occurs on cold water pipes when the air is humid. Solving this problem is simple: either wrap the pipes with an insulating tape or install a dehumidifier to re- move the airborne moisture be- fore it hits the cold pipes.

Valves

Most of the minor plumbing problems (and repairs) you will be dealing with involve valves. Most of these you are accustomed to think of as "faucets," but faucets are just specialized kinds of valves. Valves are mechanical devices used to control the flow of fluids—in this case, water. That's elementary. But understanding how a simple valve works will make it easier for you to make repairs confidently. The simplest valves in your plumbing system are the water line stop valves mentioned in the section on your water supply system.

Line Stop Valves

The most common type of stop valve used in domestic plumbing systems is the simple **globe valve**, which derives its name from the shape of the chamber that houses the mechanism. The globe valve connects to a pipe

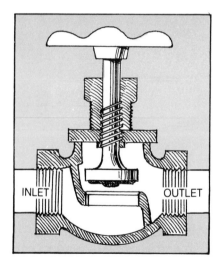

on either side. One side of the valve is the inlet—the side from which the water enters. The water then passes upward through a hole in the body of the valve and passes out through the outlet side of the valve. The handle of the valve consists of a brass **stem** that is threaded into the body of the valve so that it moves upward when turned counterclockwise; downward when the handle is turned clockwise. On the end of the stem is mounted a **washer**—nowadays usually a disc or pad of neoprene or other synthetic material which bears against the machined edge of the hole in the valve body through which the water passes on its way from the inlet to the outlet. Turning the valve handle clockwise, causing the stem to move downward and bringing the washer to bear against the rim of the hole *closes* the valve—shuts off the flow of water. Turning the handle counterclockwise reverses this chain of events and *opens* the valve.

For the valve to function properly—to shut off the water completely when closed—the washer must make firm, snug contact all the way around the machined rim of the hole in the valve body. Otherwise some water will leak through.

Now, water line stop valves are not used very often. In fact, if all goes well with the rest of the plumbing system, a stop valve may never be called into service. There is only one kind of problem likely to occur with a simple globe valve: the deterioration of the washers. In many other kinds of valves in household plumbing systems, valves are normally closed (whereas line stops are normally open) and their washers tend to become worn out from mechanical contact with the valve **seats** they bear against. In the case of globe valves, washers may simply harden through *lack* of use.

If you have never thought about your line stop valves, now is a good time to find out if they are working. Once you have figured out which valves control which areas or fixtures, shut each one in turn and check to see if they are operating properly by opening a faucet or other fixture *past* the valve. If water still comes through the faucet (or whatever) after the initial trickle of the pipe draining—that is, if a steady stream of water flows, regardless of its strength, then either you have not closed the stop valve completely, or the washer needs replacement.

The replacing of washers in globe valves is a job best left to a plumber. It takes two wrenches, plenty of leverage, and some skill and experience to loosen the *bonnet* or *packing nut* to disassemble the valve for repair. The one saving grace in calling a plumber for a repair of this kind is that, since all your line stop valves were probably installed at the same time, if one needs a new washer, they probably all do, and you can get them all taken care of at once.

Fixture Stop Valves

Many household plumbing systems, especially more up-to-date installations, provide stops for each individual fixture or appliance that uses water from the house supply. These are typically small round-handled, chrome-plated valves located where the **stub-outs** (the ends of the branch supply pipes) come out of the walls. These valves which we will refer to as **fixture stops** (but which are called, in the trade, simply **stops**), are in turn connected to the small ($\frac{1}{4}$-inch diameter) chrome-plated **sup-**

ply tubes which lead to the faucet, toilet refill valve, or other fixture mechanisms.

Fixture stops are provided as an added convenience to whomever carries out routine maintenance on faucets, etc., so it is not necessary to track down and shut off a water line stop—the shut-off can be accomplished easily on the spot. For this convenience to be a convenience, these stops, like the line stops, must work; they must shut the water off all the way. Unfortunately, the washers on many fixture stops are not replaceable, so when they stop working, as they sometimes do, the stops themselves must be replaced. Here's how.

Replacing a Fixture Stop

This book assumes that your plumbing system employs fixture stops that screw onto threaded stub-outs or are held onto unthreaded stub-outs by compression connections. If your water supply system is made from copper tubing and the fixture stop is soldered on, your problem is more complicated, and it may be time to call the plumber.

1. Turn off the *water line stop* that feeds the fixture.

2. Check to see that the water is completely turned off. If a toilet supply stop is being replaced, carefully remove the tank lid. Flush the toilet. Sponge out the remaining water from the bottom of the tank. Flush the toilet again. If a faucet supply stop is being replaced, turn on (i.e., open) the faucet for the line being worked on. After a few seconds, the water should stop dribbling from the spout. If the toilet begins to refill after the second flush or if the faucet still drips, the stop valve should have its washer replaced. Close a stop valve further back down the line or close the main valve.

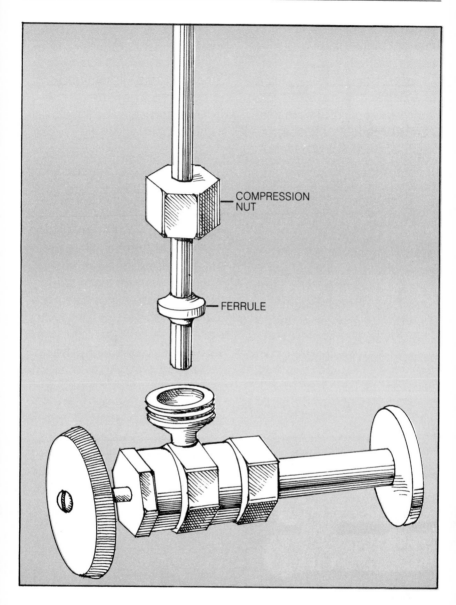

COMPRESSION
NUT

FERRULE

3. Cover the floor under the area with newspaper (to catch the water from the supply tube). Loosen the nut holding the supply tube to the faucet or toilet and the nut holding the other end of the tube to the stop valve. Remove the supply tube.

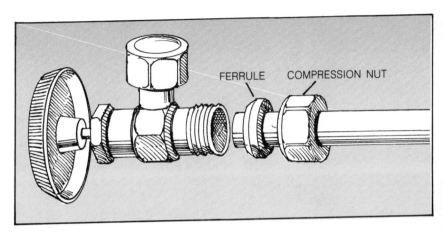

FERRULE   COMPRESSION NUT

4. Hold the stub-out with a pipe wrench, if possible, and the valve body (if you are removing a screw-on stop) or the compression nut (if you are removing a valve with compression fittings on both inlet and supply) with an adjustable wrench. Turn the valve or the nut counterclockwise until the valve is free of the stub-out.

5. Take the valve to the plumbing supply house for a replacement. Note that if you replace the stop with one of significantly different design or dimensions, you may have to replace the supply tube as well. Your dealer should be able to advise.

6. If you will have to install a new supply tube, it will first have to be cut to length. Supply tubes are quite flexible and can be bent into the necessary shape by hand. Bend the tube roughly into shape, making sure that it will enter the stop valve fairly straight, then cut it slightly overlength, using a hacksaw or a small tubing cutter. Smooth the end with a file and make sure no burrs block the tube.

7. Install the new stop valve on the stub-out. If yours is a screw-on type valve, first wrap the threads of the stub-out with a layer or two of Teflon tape **thread dope**. (The term *thread dope* originated long before Teflon tape was invented. The old standard product was a viscous gray liquid. In any case, the purpose is the same: to seal the threads and keep water from leaking out through them.) Use a wrench to screw the valve onto the stub-out

until it is reasonably snug and is oriented properly (i.e. with the supply tube connection straight up). If your stop is a compression-fit type, slip the compression nut over the stub-out, followed by the **ferrule** or compression ring. Thread the nut onto the male threads of the stop valve body after wrapping the threads with Teflon tape, and tighten with a wrench.

8. If you salvaged your old supply tube (that is, if the new stop is pretty much identical to the old) simply remove the nut and ferrule from the supply tube connection on the valve body, insert the old supply tube into the new valve and use the old nut to make the connection. In this case, you will refasten the other end of the supply tube exactly as it was before you disconnected it in step 3.

If you are installing a new supply tube, *first* slip on the nut that will attach the tube to the faucet, etc., making sure it is oriented properly (i.e., threads *facing the connection* the nut will make). Then slip on the small nut from the stop valve, followed by the ferrule. Tape the male threads on the stop valve body and tighten the nut.

9. "Pressure test" all the connections you have made by opening the water line stop or main house shut-off. If any of the connections leak, tighten the nuts involved until the leaks cease. (In the case of a leak at the joint between a screw-on stop and threaded stub-out, the supply tube will have to be detached and the valve given a complete turn with the wrench.)

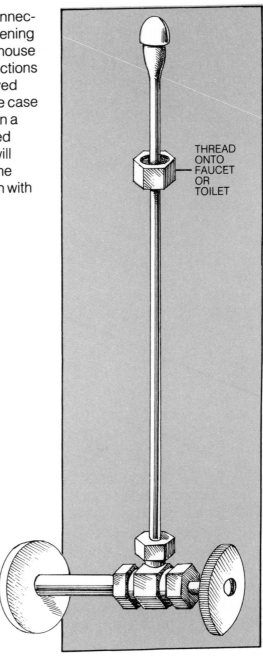

THREAD ONTO FAUCET OR TOILET

Faucets

Sink and shower faucets, too, are valves. Water comes up through pipes of the fresh water system, through the supply tubes, makes its way into the body of a faucet and then pushes up through a hole known as the valve seat. In a "compression" faucet, when the handle is in the closed position, the faucet stem, with a washer at its base, sits tightly on top of the seat, preventing water from flowing. When the handle is turned to the on position, the stem lifts the washer up above the seat, permitting water to flood through the hole and go out of the spout.

Fixing a Dripping Faucet

Most compression faucets (and that includes *most* faucets with separate controls for hot and cold water) are made of the same basic parts, though they may not always *look* alike. Some faucets have additional parts

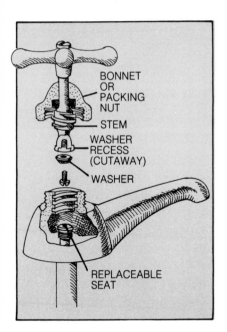

BONNET
OR
PACKING
NUT

STEM

WASHER
RECESS
(CUTAWAY)

WASHER

REPLACEABLE
SEAT

beyond the basic ones pictured here, such as an escutcheon, a set screw, a packing nut, etc. Hot water washers need to be re-

placed more frequently than cold, because the heat softens the washer and it therefore deteriorates faster. If this is going to be your maiden voyage into the plumbing realm, diagram your faucet as you take it apart so you can be sure to reassemble it properly.

Disassembling the Faucet

1. Turn off the water supply to the faucet.

2. Remove the handle. There might be a small snap-on or screw-on button in the center. Pry it off with a pocket knife (or unscrew it) and remove the screw underneath. Many handles are held to the spindle with a small set screw; if yours is, loosen the screw with either an Allen wrench or a small screwdriver. Faucet handles often need a little persuasion to be separated from the spindle. Tap from beneath and lift off.

3. If there is an escutcheon, remove it. (Escutcheons are usually held in place either by a set screw or by a hold-down nut.)

4. Unscrew the **bonnet** (also called the *stem packing nut*) with an open-end wrench or adjustable wrench.

5. Set the handle back on the spindle and use it to back off (unscrew) and lift out the stem (turn clockwise until the stem is free of the faucet body).

6. The interior of the faucet will be more or less the same whether it is the type with an integral spout or simply one handle of a "mixing" faucet, controlling the hot or cold water but leading to a common spout. Wipe out the inside of the faucet with a paper towel. Upon inspection, you'll see what looks like a brass ring surrounding the opening. This is the rim of the valve seat. Is it clean? Or is it chipped, nicked, or roughened? If it is damaged in any way, it should be replaced or redressed (see below).

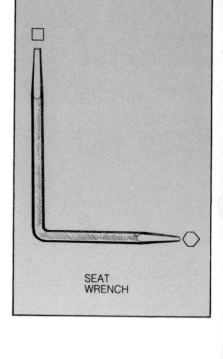

SEAT
WRENCH

Replacing a Valve Seat

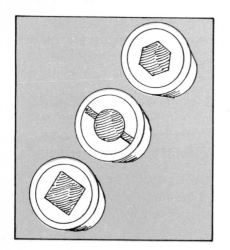

The shape of the hole in the seat will indicate if it is replaceable (see illustrations). A standard-blade screwdriver will take out the slotted seat. An Allen wrench or the hexagonal end of a seat wrench will remove a seat with a hexagonal hole and the square end of the seat wrench will extract a seat with a square hole. Take the old seat to the hardware store for comparison when buying a replacement. The new seat is simply screwed into the faucet body in place of the old one, using the appropriate tool. Tighten it snugly, but don't drive it in hard enough to damage either the threads or the opening in the seat.

Some faucets have what is called a barrel seat. They are removable, they must be reconditioned (if they are damaged) using a tool known as a seat dresser. The seat dressing tool fastens onto the faucet by threading on where the packing or bonnet nut usually sits. The

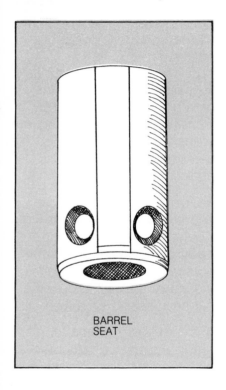

BARREL
SEAT

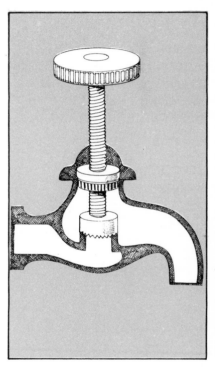

simply dropped into the faucet body rather than being screwed in. Although shaped differently than ordinary seats, they serve the same function.

Redressing a Valve Seat

If the seats in your faucets are not toothed grinding plate at the end of the tool stem then grinds a smooth surface in the soft brass rim of the seat, removing all nicks and gouges, and leaving a straight, true edge that will meet the faucet washer accurately and halt the flow of water.

After redressing a valve seat, be sure to remove all the particles of metal that you have ground off. If they are left inside a faucet body, they will soon damage the washer and you will be back to a dripping faucet in no time. One way to flush all the waste particles out of the faucet body is to *cautiously* open the fixture stop valve controlling the faucet in question and let the flow of water carry all the residue away down the sink. Close the fixture stop before you proceed with your faucet repair.

Completing Faucet Repairs

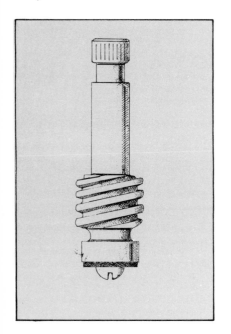

1. Remove the screw from the end of the stem and take off the worn washer. Replace it with a new washer of the *same size*. If the screw has deteriorated, replace it with a new screw of the *same length*. (If the stem looks "beaten up," try to find replacement; it will probably come with a washer and screw already attached.)

2. Reassemble the unit but do not replace the escutcheon yet. Tighten the packing or bonnet nut before you turn down the handle so that the washer sits against the seat.

3. Open the supply stop valve and turn the faucet handle to On. If water seeps from under the nut packing, tape is needed on the nut threads. If water leaks from around the stem at the top of the nut, new packing is required.

4. Close the supply stop valve again, and remove the nut and stem. Separate the stem from the nut. Depending on the design of the faucet, replace one of the following three kinds of packing: a rubber 0 ring that fits in a recess in the stem; a packing washer that sits under the nut and hugs the stem; or packing string or "self-forming" packing that also sits directly under the nut. Re-

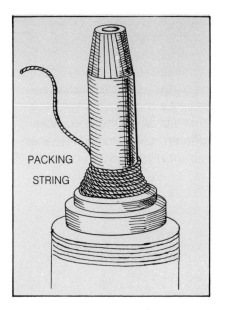

PACKING
STRING

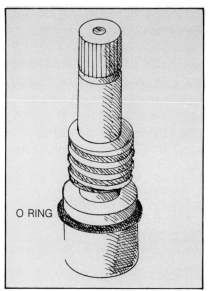

O RING

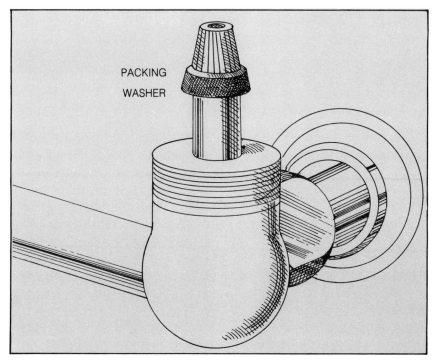

PACKING
WASHER

assemble the faucet; turn on the water to recheck for leakage; replace the escutcheon, and position the handle so that its spokes are symmetrically oriented (at a later time it will probably need readjusting).

Shower Faucets

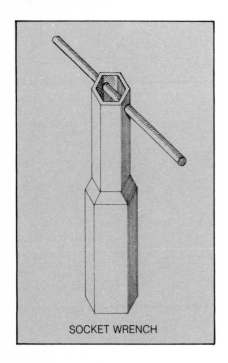

SOCKET WRENCH

Shower faucets are similar to those on a sink or lavatory. Their stems, because of the position-

ing of the faucet body in the wall behind plaster and tile, are usually quite long (see illustration page 46). Removing the stem nut may take a special large hollow tool called a socket wrench. Treat shower faucets like any other compression faucet when the shower head drips water—make sure the seats are in good condition and replace washers and packing as needed.

Single-lever Faucets

The interiors of various models of single-lever (non-compression) faucets vary considerably from manufacturer to manufacturer. Although many of the faucets look quite similar, their guts differ considerably, as do the ways the lever arms work. On some the arm swings from the top of the unit; the lever on others attaches to a pin exiting from the back of the faucet body; others have a knob-type handle that is pushed, pulled, and rotated to control mix and flow. The handle may control a "ball and cam" mechanism, a "valve and cam" assembly, or a self-contained "cartridge."

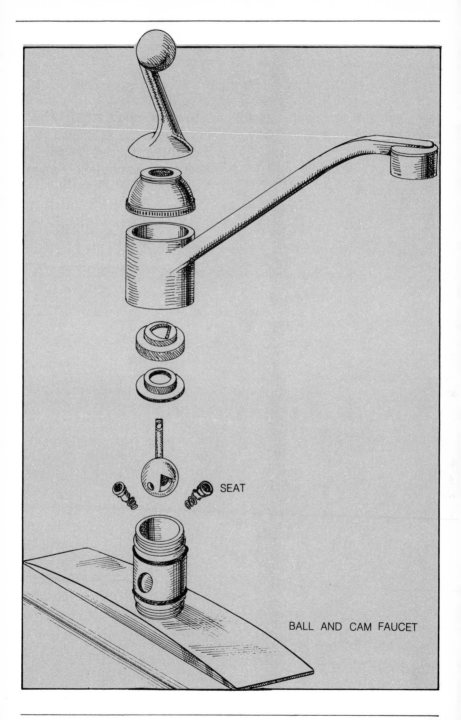

SEAT

BALL AND CAM FAUCET

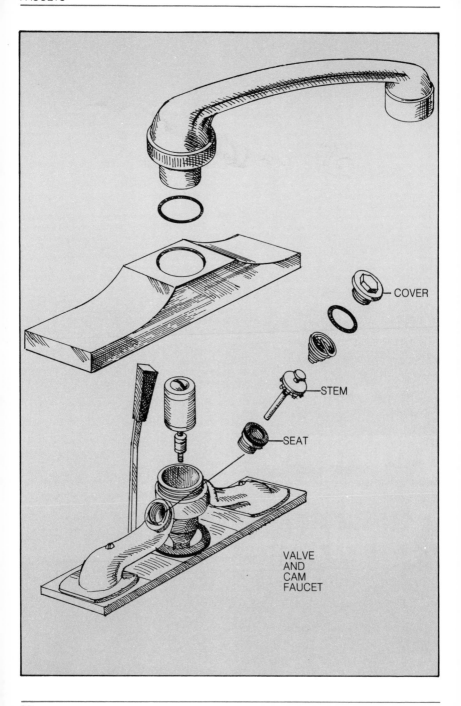

COVER

STEM

SEAT

VALVE
AND
CAM
FAUCET

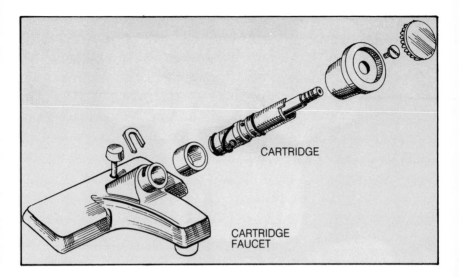

CARTRIDGE

CARTRIDGE
FAUCET

The innards of these faucets, in other words, are completely different from the compression faucet; however, repairing them is relatively simple. Instead of changing washers, seats, etc., the entire internal control assembly is usually replaced or rebuilt. Parts for the units are packaged in small kits which include diagrams and instructions for installation. Do not disassemble the faucet before you purchase replacement parts. Go to a plumbing supply house armed with the following information:

1. type of faucet (single-lever)

2. manufacturer's name (usually stamped someplace on the spout)

3. model number (sketch the unit if the model number is not visible on the fixture)

4. the particular plumbing problem—dripping spout; water seeping from under the spout; handle movement too tight, too lose, etc.

If your faucet is not among those pictured on pages 37–39, and if you do not have an assembly drawing of the unit, ask the plumbing supplier to make a copy for you from his parts catalogue.

Single-lever shower faucets generally work in the same manner as the single-lever sink faucets. The parts differ slightly in size and shape, but the principles of repairing them are exactly the same.

Sprays and Showers

S ink sprays and showers that don't have their own faucets have water channeled to them by a small part called a diverter valve. This small component does what its name says: diverts the water that ordinarily would have gone through the sink or tub spout up through the sink hose or shower riser (vertical fresh water pipe) to the spray head or shower head. How well the diverter is working is one of the factors that determines spray or shower performance. The sink spray diverter is activated by pressing the lever on the spray head and the shower diverter is engaged by pushing, pulling, or turning a lever (depending on the type of diverter). Although the diverter, when activated, is supposed to prevent water from running out of the spout, it doesn't always. Some diverters normally send a thin trickle dripping from their spouts; if a full stream pours from the spout however, the diverter needs cleaning or replacing.

Other parts of spray and shower assemblies also effect performance and should be checked before cleaning of the diverter itself is done. Sometimes a clogged aerator (at the end of the spout) or a clogged hose nozzle or shower head will need sediment and/or mineral buildups removed. Also, the hose could be kinked or the hose line could be blocked.

Cleaning an Aerator

1. Wrap leather or several layers of tape around an aerator rim.

2. Use locking pliers to unthread (turn to the left) the housing. *Do not* clamp the pliers tightly—they are capable of crushing the aerator body.

3. Disassemble the various parts and rinse under running water to wash away the accumulated sediment and debris. This is best done for screens and perforated spray plates by holding the part in question against a faucet noz-

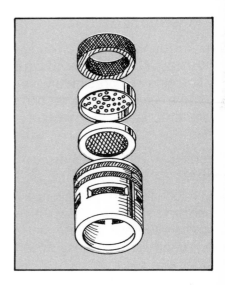

zle so that the water forces the particles back out the way they came in.

4. Reassemble the parts in order.

5. Screw the aerator back into place by hand and tighten with pliers. Take care not to over-tighten.

Cleaning a Shower Head

If the water stream coming out of a shower head is not even, the holes in the head are clogged and need to be cleaned.

1. Wrap tape or leather around the plated shower arm and hold it with a pipe wrench; similarly pro-tect the head, and use a second wrench to unscrew it from the arm.

2. Rinse out the head. Turn it opening-side-down and shake out loose particles of sand, rust, and other sediment. If the per-forations are clogged with min-eral deposits, more drastic mea-sures are called for.

3. Set the head in a pot on the stove, cover it with a mixture of half vinegar and half water, and let it simmer on the stove for at least five minutes. The vinegar will loosen the lime deposits on the inside and in the water holes. Insert a bottle brush into the opening and work it around. Rinse and dry.

4. Wrap Teflon tape on the shower arm pipe threads.

5. Replace the head, hand tight-ening it first, and then using the two wrenches tighten it securely.

Fixing a Kitchen Faucet Spray

Cleaning the Spray Nozzle

1. With a pocket knife, pry off the snap-in screw cover button.

2. Use a Phillips screwdriver to remove the screw and perfo-rated section of the nozzle.

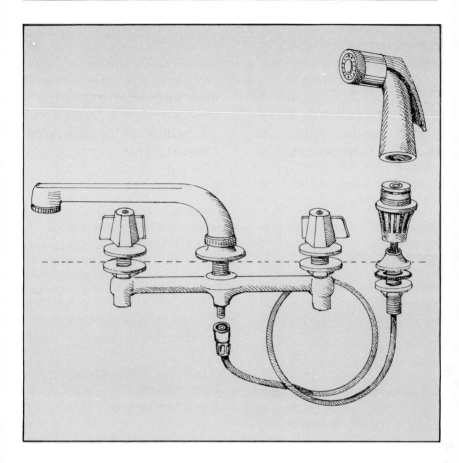

3. Set the hose in the sink and rinse accumulated sediment from the perforated plate by forcing water through the plate backwards, as with aerator parts.

4. Reassemble.

Checking for a Blocked Hose

1. Be sure the hose does not have a kink in it.

2. Separate the spray head from its knurled coupling. Grasp the coupling with one hand and turn the head counterclockwise until it detaches.

3. Park the hose in the sink temporarily and flush the spray head with water.

4. Remove both washers from the plastic endpiece on the hose and rinse clean.

5. Aim the hose into the sink and turn the water on (full blast). If the water does not run freely the hose should be replaced. If the water does run freely, reassemble the hose and check out the diverter.

Replacing a Spray Hose

1. Set a bucket on the floor (of the sink cabinet).

2. Repeat No. 2 above and remove the two washers sitting on top of the coupling.

3. Use the pocket knife to pry off the wire snap ring holding the coupling on the hose. Lift the coupling off the hose.

4. Set the hose in the sink.

5. From under the sink slowly pull the hose through the hose guide. Grab the top of the hose as it comes through the guide. Then empty the hose water into the bucket and remove the bucket.

6. The hose is connected to a short threaded nipple that projects under the faucet body. There is little clearance between the back of the cabinet (wall) and the tub of the sink in which to fit a wrench, so you may need to lie on your back under the sink. Use locking pliers or a wrench to loosen the nut that secures the

hose to the nipple. Position the pliers on the nut so that it can be turned counterclockwise to loosen it. After an initial turn or two with the tool, the nut should be loose enough to be unthreaded by hand.

7. It is a good idea to take the old hose with you when purchasing a replacement. Close the stop valve or place a note on the sink with a "Do Not Use" warning while you're gone. (A flood could greet you upon your return home if someone turns on the sink faucet.)

8. Buy a replacement unit *with* a spray and hose (even if your old spray is still in satisfactory condition, this is not an expensive purchase and it will save you time and trouble).

9. Slip the free end of the hose with the fitting through the hose guide and rest the nozzle portion in the guide.

10. Thread the hose nut over the nipple and hand tighten. Then use pliers to finish the job.

11. Turn on the water and press the spray lever to test the connection fit. Wipe the connection with a dry rag. If it leaks slightly when the water is turned on the nut requires further tightening (be careful not to *over* tighten). If there still is leakage, remove the nut and wrap Teflon tape around the nipple threads, then replace the nut and tighten.

Cleaning a Kitchen Faucet Diverter

The diverter in a kitchen sink faucet is located *in* the faucet body under the swing spout. Most diverters (self-contained, replaceable units) are inserted vertically, although a few in single-lever faucets are oriented horizontally. Their shapes vary considerably. Some lift out by pulling up on a tiny stem while others need to be unscrewed (with a screwdriver) and then lifted out.

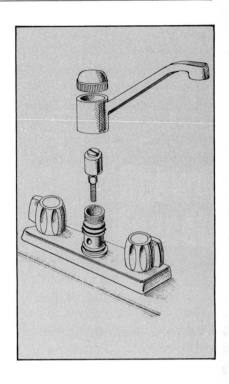

1. The spout must first be removed from the body of the faucet. Depending on the particular faucet that you have, the spout will be held on by a large cap nut, by a large threaded ring (type of nut), a long screw, etc. Cover these parts with tape or leather to protect them from the wrench, and then loosen and remove. Some spigots will lift off easily and others will need to be gently rocked loose.

2. Once the spout is off, the diverter may or may not be visible.

(Some other parts might have to be lifted out to uncover the diverter.)

3. If the diverter is the screw-in type, carefully unscrew by turning counterclockwise—just until it separates from the valve seat to which it is attached. Then lift it out. A valve with a tiny stem can be simply plucked out.

4. Take the component to *another* sink and flush water through it.

5. Cover the opening where the spout belongs with a glass (the glass should be slightly smaller than the faucet housing). Momentarily turn on both the hot and cold water—gently—to flush out residue from the faucet. (Sponge up any spilled water.)

6. Reinsert the diverter (rethread if necessary). Replace the spout and remainder of assembly.

7. Turn on the water, press the spray lever. If the water still runs heavily out of the spout, install a new diverter. Take the old diverter with you to the plumbing supply house to be sure of getting the correct replacement part.

lever tub faucet, are located on the wall by the faucet valve.

The tub diverter that has a handle of its own works like a simple stem valve. When the handle is turned, the water is redirected. Leakage around the stem should be treated as that on a stem valve (see page 34); however, if the diverting action fails, you will have to replace the entire unit.

When the tub-spout type diverter fails to work, the *spout* must be replaced with a new one of the same type.

Repairing a Shower Diverter

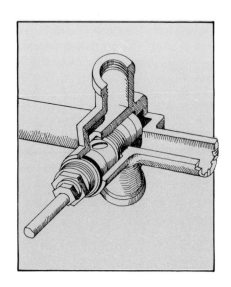

Shower diverters work on pretty much the same principle as the sink spray diverter. Some diverters have their own handles, some are situated in the tub spout, and others, in the single-

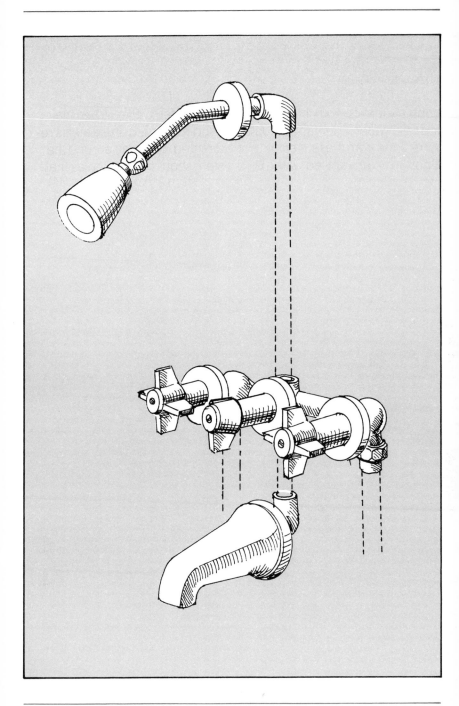

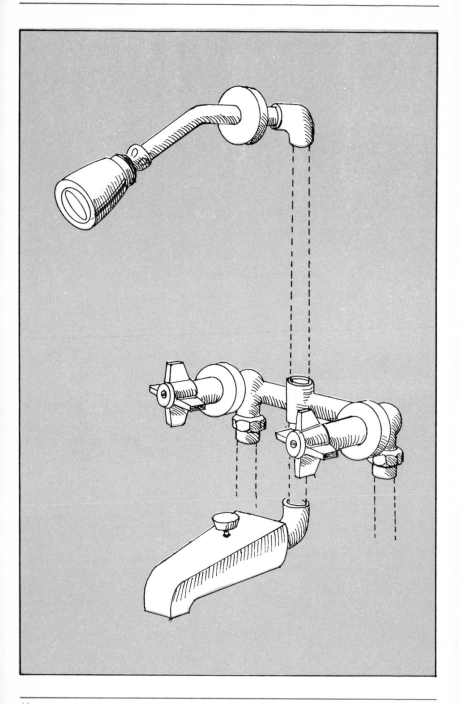

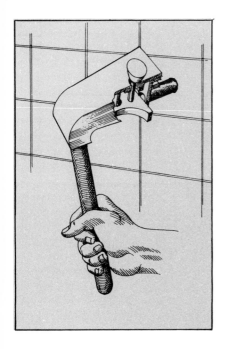

er's putty and apply it to the back exterior edge of the spout.

6. Place the spout over the nipple and engage the threads. Insert the dowel and turn clockwise to secure until the spout sits squarely in place. (The putty will make the connection against the tile watertight.)

The diverter in a single-lever faucet assembly is easily replaced, especially in those that have ball-assembly water control. Specific instructions for replacement vary from manufacturer to manufacturer. Disassemble your unit, if you can, and take the parts to your plumbing supplier who will provide you with what you need to get things working properly. If you can't figure out how to take your faucet/diverter assembly apart, note the manufacturer and model number (if you can find a model number) and ask your supplier for assistance. You may still be able to get it all done in one trip to the supply house as your supplier may be able to show you how to take your faucet apart *and* sell you the needed replacement parts—if he knows exactly which faucet you have. So, if you can't find a model number, make a sketch of the unit and take that along.

1. To remove the spout, insert a large wood dowel in the mouth of the spout (an 18″ section of an old broom handle works well).

2. Turn the dowel counterclockwise unscrewing the spout until it separates from the nipple protruding from the wall.

3. Take the spout to the plumbing supply house and purchase a replacement that is the *same length* as the old unit and employs a compatible diverter mechanism.

4. Wrap Teflon tape around the threads on the nipple.

5. Roll a ¼-inch rope of plumb-

Traps

The traps under most sinks nowadays are made of thin copper or brass tubing; in an exposed installation, the pipes are usually chrome plated. Over the years they tend to corrode and become extremely brittle. Eventually they may develop holes or cracks in the **J bend** section where water is always sitting. They may also leak at the slip nut joint connections where the pipes leading to and from the trap are secured to the J bend.

If there is a wet area on the floor below a lavatory or on the cabinet floor below the kitchen sink, track down the cause of the leak, because the J bend itself may not be at fault. A blocked pipe *beyond* the trap may be the cause of the wetness or the water may be coming from another part of the sink.

1. Check around the large slip nuts to see if there is moisture around them. If there is, the nuts need to be tightened.

2. If the slip nut joints are dry, check around the large nut under the sink that holds the faucet flange to the sink. More plumber's putty may be needed under the pop-up flange to make the flange-tailpiece assembly (the pipe making up the top part of the drain pipe) watertight. Also, the large nut may need to be tightened.

3. If none of the above areas proves to be the source of trouble, there are two other possibilities to check. In a kitchen sink with a spray, water could have splashed through the hose guide in the faucet body; the hose could have a hole in it; or the spray head could be leaking. All of these things would leave a puddle on the cabinet floor.

Once you have ascertained exactly what the problem is, you can easily correct it. Don't worry about water dripping through the guide hole or down the rod— these really are not plumbing problems, only people problems. If the water here continues to drip, the only thing to do is tell the members of your household to be more careful or put a small plastic container under the sink to catch these occasional drips. Of course, the dripping hose should be replaced (see page 44). If, through your investigations, you find that the trap *is* worn or broken or the connections are leaking, proceed with one of the following two repairs.

Tightening a Leaking Slip Nut

1. Set a bucket on the floor beneath the trap.

2. Use two large wrenches to tighten the nut—with a pipe wrench *carefully* hold the area adjacent to the nut (remember that the pipe is very thin-walled). Use a monkey or adjustable wrench or pump pliers on the nut itself. Be sure to wrap tape or a strip of leather under the area the pipe wrench will hold; also do the same if pump pliers are used on the nut. The pipe wrench is used only to steady the pipe while leverage is exerted clockwise on the nut.

3. Pour water down the drain and recheck the area for leakage; if it still is wet, replace the two wrenches and exert counterclockwise leverage to loosen the nut.

4. Move the nut away from the joint.

5. Clean the joint with a rag and, if necessary, steel wool.

6. Wrap Teflon tape around pipe threads.

7. The washer that was sitting under the nut probably has been dislodged, put it back into place and set the nut over it.

8. Again using both wrenches, tighten the nut. [Do not be surprised if one or both of the pipes that make up the trap develops a crack when you tighten or loosen a nut. Age just makes them very brittle and any movement can

cause the metal to snap. If this does happen, replace both the J bend and the **waste tube** (the second pipe that makes up the trap). Nuts and washers are supplied with new pipes.]

Replacing a Trap

1. Put an empty bucket under the trap.

2. Loosen both slip nuts. To remove the J bend, pull it downward.

3. Loosen the remaining slip nut that holds the waste tube to the drain line. The tube will have to be wriggled out of the drain pipe.

4. Take the J bend and waste tube to the plumbing supply house and procure replacements for both pipes.

5. Clean the threads on the drain pipe that protrudes from the wall or floor. Wrap joint tape around the threads.

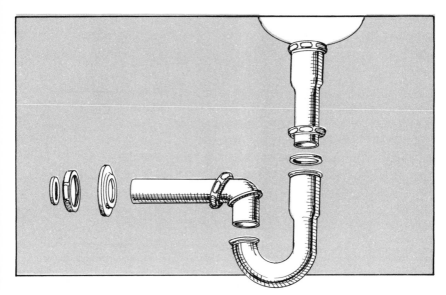

6. Slide the escutcheon, slip nut and rubber washer over the drain-connection end of the waste pipe and a second slip nut and washer over the trap-connection end.

7. Insert the proper end of the waste pipe into the drain pipe and hand-tighten the slip nut.

8. Slide the remaining slip nut and washer over the sink tailpiece. (This washer is somewhat smaller than the others to fit the diameter of the tailpiece.)

9. Wrap Teflon tape over the threads on the longer arm of the J bend.

10. Push the longer arm of the J bend over the tailpiece and work it up over the pipe as high as it will go. Loosely hand-tighten the slip nut to the J bend.

11. Rotate the J bend until the other end aligns with the waste tube. (This might take a bit of maneuvering.)

12. Wrap Teflon tape over the threads of the J bend-waste tube joint.

13. Slide the washer down to the joint, then the nut. Hand-tighten the nut.

14. Be sure all the pipes are aligned properly, then tighten all nuts, using two wrenches.

15. Turn on the water and test the joints to see that they are watertight.

Clogged Drains

Slow or clogged drains constitute the biggest plumbing headache a homeowner encounters. People are very careless and throw garbage down the kitchen sink trap, residue collects on the walls of the pipes, and then the diameter closes in. Children revel in filling a toilet bowl with toilet paper; an overflowing toilet results. Any excess material thrown or dropped down a drain or toilet can get caught in the line and cause a blockage. The bend in a trap has a short radius and objects such as combs, toothbrushes, silverware, etc. cannot pass through the pipe.

Usually a plunger will help clear a clogged drain line; however, if something the length of a spoon is dropped down a drain, *don't* use a plunger. Instead remove the trap (see page 52) and hope that the item is lodged in it.

If you have been negligent about keeping the strainer for the kitchen sink in place, plenty of garbage probably has gone down the drain. The trap and drain pipes could become blocked from the continual addition of fats and coffee grinds to the drain. Grease tends to build up in the pipes, and coffee grinds, in turn, stick to the grease. Several repetitions of this and the line will become stuffed.

Clearing a Slow Drain

1. Remove any vegetable peelings, utensils, etc., sitting in the sink.

2. Lift out the strainer (that should be) sitting over the trap.

3. Put several pots of water on the stove to boil.

4. Wait until the water remaining in the sink empties.

5. Pour the hot water into the drain (be careful not to splash yourself).

6. If there was no tight blockage, the water should have dissolved some of the material sticking to the inside of the waste pipe and allowed the water to run freely through the line.

7. If steps 1-6 were successful, open the hot water tap and let it run for several minutes.

If the line is still sluggish, use a *homemade* drain cleaner.

1. After the water has emptied from the sink, pour one cup of baking soda followed by one cup of vinegar down the drain.

2. Immediately replace the strainer in the closed position or plug the opening with a wet cloth. The reaction of the bicarbonate of soda and acetic acid (vinegar) sets up a bubbly chemical action.

3. Leave the drain tightly covered for 15–20 minutes.

4. If the soda/vinegar succeeds in opening the pipe, continue to flush it by running hot tap water for several minutes.

Using a Plunger

1. Clear the sink of all but a few inches of water.

2. Lift out the strainer.

3. Set the cup of the plunger over the drain mouth and, with both hands on the handle, forcefully pump up and down several times.

4. If the water goes down the drain when the plunger is lifted from the top of the sink, replace the plunger and add more water. Repeat Steps 1–3.

5. Follow by running hot tap water for several minutes.

Toilets

The toilet is thought, by many, to be a mysterious contraption. It can cause innumerable plumbing troubles when its innards are not in A-1 condition: it can be noisy, use an excessive amount of water, flush too slowly, overflow, etc. Once you actually know how it works, it won't be difficult to find exactly where the problems lie and repair or replace the worn part(s).

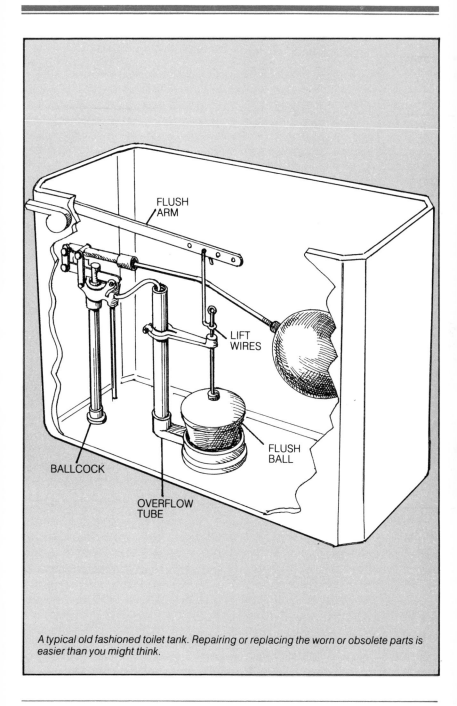

FLUSH ARM

LIFT WIRES

BALLCOCK

FLUSH BALL

OVERFLOW TUBE

A typical old fashioned toilet tank. Repairing or replacing the worn or obsolete parts is easier than you might think.

To begin, study the illustration. The inside of an older toilet tank will be different in some respects from a newer one. Some basic parts have been completely re-designed and some have been dispensed with altogether. Where the old ballcock (refill valve) was made out of several metal parts for example, the new ones are made primarily of plastic.

To repair parts of the flushing mechanism you need to understand how it works. There are three main components of any standard tank toilet: a **refill valve** (traditionally called a "ballcock" because of the float ball used as a shut-off device); a **flush valve** consisting of a **valve seat** set in the bottom of the tank, a **stopper ball** that fits into the seat and an **overflow tube**; and a **flush handle** with some linkage to the stopper ball.

When you flush the toilet by pushing the flush handle, the stopper ball (or modern equivalent) is pulled free of the flush valve seat and the tank empties into the toilet bowl, carrying the contents of the bowl down the soil line. As the water level drops in the tank, the refill valve is opened and fresh water flows into the tank. As the water level reaches the bottom of the tank, the stopper ball, which has been riding on the surface of the water since it was pulled free of the seat is drawn back into the flush valve seat by the siphon action of the water leaving the tank. This ends the flushing action. The toilet tank continues to refill until the valve is closed by the action of the floating ball and arm (or its modern equivalent). During the tank refill stage, the water level in the toilet bowl is brought up to the the proper level by a little refill tube that empties into the overflow tube. This refill is connected to the refill valve and shuts off when it does. This completes the flush cycle.

The two most common toilet problems are different versions of the same basic trouble: constantly running water. The first results when the stopper ball does not make a complete seal with the flush valve seat. The other is a refill valve that never quite shuts off. In the case of the former problem, you should hear the refill valve go into action briefly from time to time, to bring the water in the tank up to the proper level. If you have the second problem, the malfunctioning refill valve, you may or may not be able to detect it by ear. Two telltale signs are: the water level in the tank is up to the top of the overflow tube; or a barely visible movement of water in the toilet bowl from overflow.

Faulty Stopper Ball or Seat

To check for a malfunctioning stopper ball or flush valve seat, first close the supply stop valve and flush the toilet to empty the tank. Sponge up the excess water in the bottom of the tank, then check parts as follows:

1. Does the stopper ball sit tightly in the valve seat? The ball and seat must line up correctly in order to achieve a proper fit. The bracket that guides the lift wires might need slight adjustment to redirect the wires so that the ball drops snugly into place.

2. Unthread and remove the stopper ball and shine a flashlight into the flush valve seat. Examine it for corrosion and residue buildup. Remove them by scouring with steel wool; then wipe clean with a rag.

3. Wash off the stopper ball. Is it mushy feeling, or has it broken out with "pimples?" Rubber does soften and wear out—especially when it sits constantly in water. Replace a worn stopper ball or install the newer "Flapper" type that uses a cord or chain instead of a lift wire.

4. To install a flapper, first remove the guide bracket, lift rod and lift wire from the overflow tube. Slide the new unit into place over the overflow tube, positioning it carefully. Tighten the securing screw or clamp, if any, to hold the flap-

Two types of modern "flapper" flush balls.

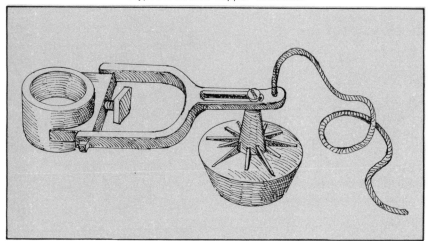

per permanently in place. Hook or tie the lift cord or chain to the trip lever.

5. Whichever type of ball you are using, to achieve a better seal, wipe the valve seat and the bottom of the ball with a thin coat of petroleum jelly. This should end valve seat leakage for good.

Faulty Refill Shut-off

In investigating the function of the refill valve, begin by doing a bit of detective work. First, remove (unscrew) the float ball and shake it. Does it have water in it? The slightest amount of water in the float ball will make it ineffective in shutting off the valve and there will be continually running water. If there is a visible leak in the ball, replace it.

Second, if the float arm is adjusted for too high a water cut-off level, the lever will rise above the overflow tube and water will constantly run down the tube. If the water level is up this high and the float ball seems to be riding high in the water, try bending the float arm downward a bit. Use both hands to make the bend. (Hold the rod with one hand to take the strain off the lever piece on the ballcock and bend the arm downward with the other hand.) It takes only a very slight adjustment to change the water level. If that adjustment takes care of the problem, great. But if the water is still running, chances are that the internal mechanism of the valve is not functioning properly.

You can rebuild the ballcock or replace it. If you decide to rebuild, you can obtain a valve rebuild kit from your plumbing supplier that should come with full instructions for replacing the necessary parts. But nowadays, the newly designed refill valve assemblies are considerably more reliable than the older metal ones, so why not consider replacing the whole unit? The parts should cost under $10.

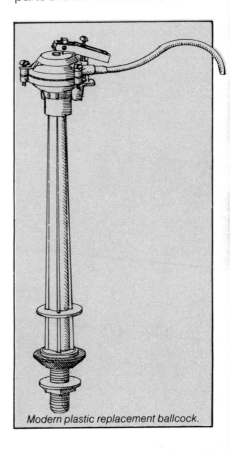

Modern plastic replacement ballcock.

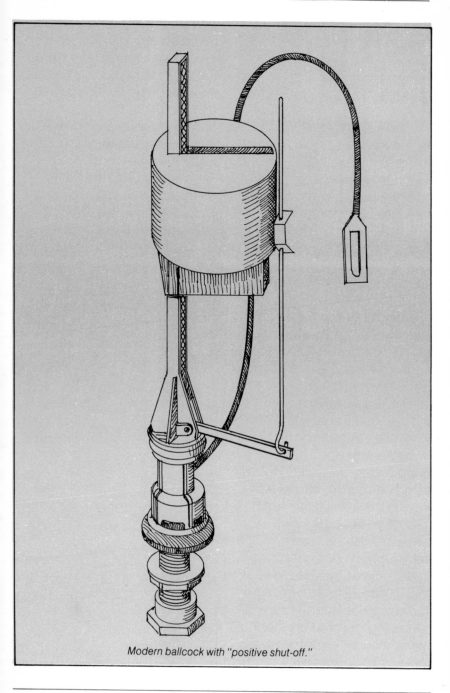

Modern ballcock with "positive shut-off."

Replacing a Worn Ballcock

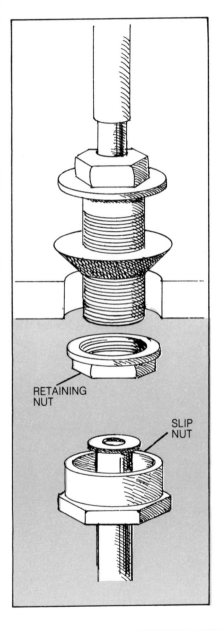

RETAINING NUT

SLIP NUT

1. Shut off the supply stop valve (this must be a *tight* shutoff or you will have a flood.

2. Set a bucket under the connection.

3. Flush the toilet and sponge out the remaining water.

4. Remove the float arm and float ball.

5. With and adjustable wrench, loosen the large slip nut holding the supply tube to the ballcock. Separate the tube from the unit.

6. Slip a large wrench over the nut at the base of the ballcock. This will keep the unit from rotating as the nut under the tank is loosened.

7. Working counterclockwise, loosen the nut holding the ballcock to the tank. Work with care since the vitreous china tank will crack with little pressure. If necessary, soak the joint with penetrating oil. Then use a hammer to tap, not smash, the handle of the wrench. If the nut still will not budge, call a plumber.

The new unit is packed with all necessary washers, gaskets, and nuts. Clean the base of the tank before installing the new ballcock.

The Wallaby Home Care Guides

How to Fix a Leak and Other Household
Plumbing Projects

How to Redo Your Kitchen Cabinets and
Counter Tops

How to Wallpaper

How to Paint Interiors

How to Build a Deck

How to Wire Electrical Outlets, Switches and
Lights

The Wallaby Auto Care Guides

How to Tune Your Chevy Chevette

How to Tune Your Toyota Corolla